Mammal Misfits

Mammal Misfits

Sara Swan Miller

Watts LIBRARY

Franklin Watts
A Division of Grolier Publishing
New York • Hong Kong • Sydney
Danbury, Connecticut

Note to readers: Definitions for words in **bold** can be found in the Glossary at the back of this book.

Photographs ©: Animals Animals: 44 (Stephen Dalton), cover (Paul Freed), 32 (Raymond A. Mendez); Auscape: 48 (Jean-Paul Ferrero), 5 bottom, 18, 19, 21 (David Parer & Elizabeth Parer-Cook); Bat Conservation International, Inc./Merlin D. Tuttle: 10, 45; Peter Arnold Inc.: 34 (Y. Arthus-Bertrand), 17 (John Cancalosi), 42 (S.J. Krasemann), 6, 9 (Gerard Lacz), 50 (Kevin Schafer), 28, 29, 47 (Roland Seitre), 24 (Norbert Wu), 38 (Gunter Ziesler); Photo Researchers: 27 (John Bova), 40 (Nigel J. Dennis), 31 (Gregory G. Dimijian, M.D.), 2 (François Gohier), 5 top, 22 (Richard Hutchings), 11 (Bud Lehnhausen), 12 (James M. McCann), 14 (Tom McHugh), 26 (N. Smythe); Visuals Unlimited/John D. Cunningham: 37.

The photograph on the cover shows an armadillo. The photograph opposite the title page shows a blue whale, the world's largest mammal.

Visit Franklin Watts on the Internet at:
http://publishing.grolier.com

Library of Congress Cataloging-in-Publication Data

Miller, Sara Swan
    Mammal Misfits / by Sara Swan Miller
       p.   cm.— (Watts Library)
    Includes bibliographical references and index.
    Summary: Describes several species of mammals that have unusual appearances, habitats, or behaviors.
    ISBN 0-531-11795-2 (lib. bdg.)   0-531-13984-0 (pbk.)
    1. Mammals—Juvenile literature. [1. Mammals.] I. Title. II. Series.
QL706.2. M56   2000
599—dc21   99-057019

Contents

Tigers are typical land mammals

Chapter One

What Is a Mammal?

Do you know what a mammal is? People are mammals. So are polar bears and pigs, but goldfish, grasshoppers, and geese are not mammals. Cows and cats are mammals, while crocodiles are not. What's the difference between these animals? What makes an animal a mammal? Scientists organize living things into categories according to specific similarities and differences. If you've learned about mammals, you may know some things that separate them from animals in the

7

other groups, or **classes**. If some teacher asked you, "What is a mammal?" What would you say?

You might start out by saying that a mammal is a **warm-blooded vertebrate** covered with hair. That means that a mammal can control its own body temperature without needing to warm up in the sun, and that it has a backbone. A mammal's hair keeps it warm, protects it from sunburn, and sometimes acts as **camouflage**.

You might also say that before it is born, a baby mammal grows inside its mother's **uterus** (YOO-tuhr-uhs). Each mammal **embryo** is attached to a **placenta** (pluh-SENT-uh). This is a structure full of blood vessels that supplies the embryo with nutrients and oxygen from its mother.

After they are born, the babies feed on milk from their mother's body. Female mammals have **mammary glands** on the underside of their bodies. Those mammary glands produce milk for their babies.

Everything in Its Place

All living things can be classified into different categories depending on their characteristics. Plants and animals are in two different categories called **kingdoms**. Those top-level categories are divided into many smaller subcategories. As the categories get smaller, the members of each category have more features in common. Mammals make up one class of living things, a middle level category. Other animal classes are insects, reptiles, amphibians, and birds. The science of organizing living things into such categories is called **taxonomy**.

Mammals have different kinds of feet adapted to the kind of life they lead. Fast-running animals, such as horses, run swiftly on the tips of their toes, which are protected by a hoof. Meat-eaters, such as tigers, have strong, sharp claws for grabbing and holding their prey. Digging mammals, including badgers, have strong, oversized claws to help them burrow. Monkeys and some other primates have hands that are just right for grasping tree branches.

Mammals have teeth that are suited to the food they eat. Rodents have **incisors** in the front for gnawing and molars farther back for grinding their food. Mammals that eat grass,

Wolves' teeth are well suited to tearing up prey.

including horses and cows, have strong front teeth and flat molars. Meat-eaters have sharp **canine teeth** behind their incisors that help hold their prey. They also have pointed **carnassial teeth** behind their canine teeth for tearing up meat.

If you knew all that, your teacher would be pleased—but your answer wouldn't be completely right. Do *all* mammals give birth to live young? Do they *all* have fur, or teeth? The surprising answer is no!

The Smallest Mammal

Kitti's hog-nosed bat in Thailand is the size of a large bumblebee. It weighs less than a nickel!

The Biggest Mammal

The huge blue whale can grow as long as 100 feet (33 meters)— about the distance from home plate to first base on a baseball field. It can weigh more than 143 tons. That's one massive mammal!

Many mammals, from platypuses to armadillos to ant-eaters, don't look the way mammals are "supposed" to look or act the way we expect mammals to act. Let's get to know some of these strange and marvelous mammals.

Like most mammals, brown bears give birth to live young.

Chapter Two

Can a Mammal Lay Eggs?

People expect mammals to give birth to live babies. It's hard to believe that an animal can lay eggs and still be a mammal, but both the platypuses and the echidnas (ih-KID-nuhz) do just that. Remember that when it comes to mammals and their young, the one thing that all mammals have in common is that they all have mammary glands that produce

13

milk for their young. Even though the platypuses and echidnas lay eggs, scientists say that they are mammals because they feed their young with mother's milk.

Scientists put platypuses and echidnas in their own special subcategory of the mammals. These strange mammals are the only ones that lay eggs. This subcategory, or **order**, is called the **monotremes**. There are only three species of monotremes—the duck-billed platypus, the short-beaked echidna, and the long-beaked echidna. All three are found only in Australia and nearby islands.

The Duck-Billed Platypuses

About 200 years ago, someone brought a platypus to England. Scientists there thought the people showing them the strange-looking animal must be playing a trick. The platypus had

A platypus probes for food with its sensitive bill.

webbed feet, the bill of a duck, the flat tail of a beaver, and the fur of an otter. Plus, it laid eggs. Was it a bird or a mammal?

The platypus may be the strangest mammal in the world, but its odd shape is well suited to its lifestyle. It spends most of its time hunting underwater or hiding in burrows in a riverbank. The webbing between its toes helps it swim swiftly through a river. When a platypus digs, that webbing is tucked safely away under its feet.

A platypus is awkward on land, but very graceful in the water. Its body is sleek and streamlined, and its webbed feet and flat tail help it swim. When a platypus dives, folds of skin cover and protect its ears and eyes. A platypus can even close off its nostrils, so water doesn't get in. A platypus can stay underwater up to 5 minutes!

At dawn and dusk, a platypus hunts for worms, shellfish, insects, and other small animals. A platypus's leathery bill has lots of nerves in it and is very sensitive. As a platypus swims over the river bottom, it swings its head from side to side. When it feels prey with its bill, the platypus scoops it up and stores it in pouches in its cheeks. Then it comes up to the surface to eat and catch a breath of air.

The platypus has no teeth. Instead, it has horny pads in the back of its mouth that help it grind up its food. Mud and gravel scooped up with its prey help to crush food between the pads.

When the Australian spring comes, it's mating time for the platypuses. Females go looking for males. When a female

Where in the World are Platypuses?

Platypuses live only in the lakes and streams of southern and eastern Australia and Tasmania.

During the day, they hide in burrows. They mainly come out at dawn and dusk to hunt.

finds one, the male holds onto her tail, and they swim around in circles.

After they mate, the female prepares a nesting burrow. She digs a tunnel nearly 50 feet (15 m) long into the riverbank. Then she digs a "room" at the end of the tunnel and lines it with leaves. Just before she lays her eggs, she plugs the tunnel entrance with mud, leaves, and grass. Now she and her eggs will be safe.

The female platypus lays one or two small, leathery eggs in the nest. The eggs are sticky and cling to the mother's fur. For 10 days she stays curled around the eggs, rarely leaving the burrow. During this time, the female mainly lives off the fat stored in her tail.

By the end of the **incubation period**, there is very little oxygen left in the burrow. Luckily, the platypus can store oxygen in its blood, so it can survive until the young hatch.

The newly hatched babies are only 1 inch (2.5 centimeters) long. Their bills are soft, so that they can lick milk from patches on their mother's belly. The mother has no nipples, just **pores** that the milk flows out of.

It takes nearly 3 months for the babies' eyes to open. During that time, the hungry mother dashes out of her

Pocket Babies

Most female mammals carry their young inside their bodies before the babies are born. Each embryo is attached to a placenta, which provides nutrients and oxygen from the mother's blood and carries off waste products. The placenta nourishes the embryo inside its mother's body until the baby is ready to be born.

Some mammals, the **marsupials** (mahr-SOUP-ee-uhls), don't have placentas. A marsupial embryo is born long before it is able to survive outside the mother's body. The tiny embryo has to climb from the birth canal to its mother's pouch. The mother licks a trail in her belly fur for it to follow. Once in the pouch, the embryo latches onto a nipple and lives on its mother's milk for several more weeks or months.

Some marsupials, such as the numbat, have no pouch. A numbat mother has long fur on her belly that protects her baby. Once a newborn numbat latches onto a nipple, it hangs on for dear life!

burrow now and then, feeds quickly and then comes back to nurse her young. When their eyes finally open, the young platypuses practice swimming. They stay close to the opening of the burrow in the riverbank, and hunt for worms and other prey. It will be another 3 months before they are ready to go off on their own.

A platypus has another claim to fame—it is the only mammal that produces poisonous **venom**. The male has sharp spurs on his hind feet with a tube connected to a poison gland. The platypus uses its spurs for defense.

A Look at Echidnas

The short-beaked echidna, which lives in Australia, looks like a spiny football with feet and a long, pointy nose that scientists call a "beak."

In July and August—the Australian winter—short-beaked echidnas get ready to mate. One female waddles along, followed by a group of males walking in single file. It's an "echidna train!" The males may follow the female for up to 6 weeks before she's ready to mate. Then she chooses one male from the train. The others are out of luck.

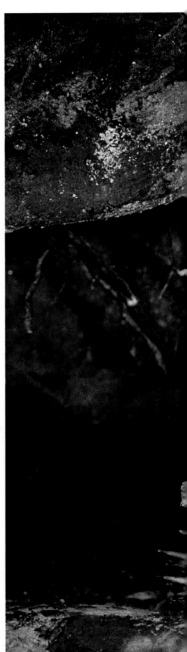

After mating, the female lays an egg the size of a small grape in a pouch on her belly. A few weeks later, the leathery egg hatches inside the female's pouch. The newborn echidna is no bigger than a raisin and is almost entirely helpless. It has neither hair nor claws, and it can't see. It finds a milk patch on

A young short-beaked echidna in its burrow.

its mother's belly, latches onto it, and begins to nurse. Amazingly, an echidna's milk is pink!

The baby stays inside its mother's pouch for nearly 2 months, nursing and growing. When it begins to grow spines, its days in the pouch are over. The mother digs a burrow and leaves the baby there. Every few days, she comes back to nurse it. Finally, when it is 1 year old, the baby is ready to survive on its own.

Echidnas are slow-moving, but they have a good way to protect themselves from enemies. When something scares an echidna, it digs straight down into the ground and buries itself until only its spines stick up. Then it curls up in a tight ball and hangs onto underground rocks with its strong claws. No **predator** wants a mouthful of sharp spines!

Like platypuses, male echidnas have sharp spurs on their hind feet. Echidna spines don't contain venom—but those sharp points make picking up an echidna a risky move!

This baby short-beaked echidna has no spines yet.

Like this girl and her dog, most mammals have fur.

Chapter Three

Where's Your Fur?

When you think of a mammal, you probably picture a furry animal such as a cat or dog. It's true that most mammals have fur. If the earliest mammals didn't have fur, they could never have survived when dinosaurs roamed the planet. Being warm-blooded and having fur to keep warm meant that mammals could come out to search for food on chilly nights. Dinosaurs and other reptiles had to warm up in the sun before they could move around, so they weren't out hunting at night. Being **nocturnal** helped the earliest mammals avoid these big reptile predators.

Most modern mammals are still nocturnal, and most have kept their fur. Some of them, though, have very little fur. Some have armor or scales instead of fur. Some are almost entirely naked!

The Banded Armadillo

An armadillo doesn't look like a mammal at all. The name "armadillo" means "little armored animal" in Spanish. The famous naturalist John James Audubon said an armadillo looks like a pig in a turtle's shell. At first glance you might think it really was a turtle. Then you might notice a few hairs

An armadillo looks like a cross between a pig and a turtle.

sprouting out between parts of its **carapace**, or protective armor. The armadillo's carapace is a double layer of horn and bone that covers the animal's back and sides.

When an armadillo is born, it has soft, shiny skin and a pale pink carapace. After a few days, its carapace gets harder. For the first few months, the carapace stays soft and flexible so that the young armadillo has room to grow. After 2 or 3 months in its leafy nest, though, its carapace hardens. Once it has the safety of this protective armor, the young armadillo is ready to go off on its own.

Armadillos live in the southern United States and in Central and South America. During warm weather, they stay inside their shady burrows during the day and come out in the cool evening to look for food. Having a carapace instead of hair makes armadillos very sensitive to the temperature. The hot sun could roast them inside their armor. In colder weather, armadillos stay warm inside their burrows at night and come out during the warmer daylight hours. A carapace isn't as good as a furry coat for keeping an animal warm on a cold night.

Armadillos have tiny eyes and poor vision. They don't hear well either. However, they have an excellent sense of smell. An armadillo can smell a beetle hiding 7 inches (18 cm) underground. The armadillo's sense of smell is its best tool for hunting food.

An armadillo has many enemies, but it also has many ways of protecting itself. Its carapace is its best defense. The armor grows in bands around the armadillo's body, so it is quite

The Smallest Armadillo

It's hard to tell whether a pink fairy armadillo is coming or going. How do you know which end is which? The pointed end is its head. Its snout is covered with soft, white hair. The tail end is wider and has a short fringe of hair.

The pink fairy armadillo is the smallest armadillo in the world. It is only 5 to 6 inches (12.5 to 15 cm) long. It's an excellent digger, though. It digs a burrow to hide in during the day and comes out at night to feed, mostly on ants. Usually, a pink fairy armadillo digs its burrow near anthills. Then it can be close to its food supply.

flexible. A three-banded armadillo can roll itself into a tight ball. When an armadillo snaps shut like a trap, it's almost impossible for a predator to pry it open.

A nine-banded armadillo can't roll itself into a ball, but it has other ways to defend itself. For example, it can run surprisingly quickly. If a coyote or another enemy gets too close, the armadillo can jump straight up into the air, letting the coyote run underneath it. Once the coyote has passed by, the armadillo quickly digs itself into the soil. An armadillo can dig itself to safety in 2 minutes, and once it digs in, almost no enemy can dig it out.

Sadly, none of these defenses can protect an armadillo from its newest enemies—trucks and cars! If an armadillo tries to protect itself by rolling up in a ball, the car will squish it. Leaping up in the air doesn't work, either. The animal ends up leaping into the path of the oncoming car. Not even a

Watch out for cars! A nine-banded armadillo crosses the road.

fast-digging armadillo can dig to safety on a road. So, every year, cars and trucks kill thousands of armadillos.

What Is a Pangolin?

Is that a big lizard digging in that termite mound? The animal is covered with scales, and when it walks away, it drags a long, lizard-like tail behind it. It certainly doesn't look like a mammal! Pangolins (pang-GOH-luhnz) are the only mammals with scales. They may look like lizards, but they are mammals. They are warm-blooded and give birth to live young. Most

This Malayan pangolin is searching for insects.

importantly, like all other mammals, pangolins feed their young with mother's milk.

A young pangolin rides on its mother's back.

A newborn pangolin may weigh only 7 ounces (200 grams), and its scales are small and soft. A full-grown adult pangolin is well protected by tough, overlapping scales that cover most of its body, including its long tail. The mother curls her scaly body around her young to keep it safe. When the baby gets bigger, it rides about on its mother's back, holding onto her scales with its sharp claws. As the young pangolin ages, its scales harden. Eventually it is able to protect itself.

The pangolin has a lot of enemies, including lions and leopards. Fortunately, it can take care of itself. A pangolin's scales are made of the same material as your fingernails, and

The seven species of pangolins live in the warm parts of Africa and southern Asia. The smallest, the long-tailed pangolin of Africa, measures 24 inches (60 cm) from its nose to the tip of its long tail.

The largest, the giant pangolin of Africa, is about 5 feet (1.5 m) long. Sadly, pangolins are becoming rare. People kill them for their meat and hides and destroy their forest homes for farmland.

the edges of these scales are very sharp. When a predator attacks, a pangolin curls up in a tight ball and wraps its tail around its body to protect its soft belly. Then it raises the sharp edges of its scales to ward off its attacker. It's nearly impossible to uncurl a rolled-up pangolin!

Ants and termites are the pangolin's favorite foods. These insects live in large nests and mounds with hard clay walls that are almost impossible to break into. The pangolin is well equipped to deal with the mounds, however. It has large, strong claws that can break through the hard walls. Then the animal sticks its incredibly long, sticky tongue inside and slurps up the insects.

A pangolin's mouth is very strange. There are no teeth inside. In order to crush and grind the insects it eats, the pangolin swallows tiny pebbles. Inside the animal's stomach, those pebbles help to grind up its meal. Another amazing feature is the pangolin's tongue, which is two-thirds as long as its body. The pangolin's long, sticky tongue can reach insects 12 inches (30 cm) away. Using its unusual feeding tools, one pangolin can eat as many as 200,000 ants a night.

Naked Mole Rats

Naked mole rats have almost no hair at all. These peculiar-looking mammals have wrinkled pink and purple skin. The skin on their bellies is nearly transparent. If you look closely, though, you will see that a naked mole rat does have a few hairs. It is nearly blind, but it uses whiskers on its face and tail to feel its way around in the underground tunnels where it lives. Between the animal's toes are short hairs that it uses like a broom to sweep the soil away.

Naked mole rats are only about 3.5 inches (8.5 cm) long, and weigh 1 to 2 ounces (28 to 57 gm). They live in big

Naked mole rats live in large groups.

Where in the World Are Naked Mole Rats?

These underground mammals are hard to find. They live only in the African countries of Kenya, Ethiopia, and Somalia.

A naked mole rat uses its teeth to dig a tunnel.

colonies. Usually there are about 70 animals living together in a burrow, but sometimes a colony may have as many as 300 members. You would think naked mole rats would get cold, but the air temperature and humidity in the burrows never changes very much. It is always about 88 degrees Fahrenheit (31 degrees Celsius), with 90 percent humidity. The mole rats' bare skin soaks up the warmth, so they don't need fur to stay warm. Huddling together also helps keep them warm.

To dig their underground tunnels, naked mole rats work as a relay team. The first animal in line digs through the soil with its powerful front teeth. Behind it, a series of workers sweep the soil backward up the tunnel and eventually kick it outside.

When the first rat has dug up a lot of soil, it backs up through the tunnel, pushing out the soil with its hind feet. Then the next animal in line takes over the digging.

The burrows these mammals create are large and complex. The tunnels often branch into other tunnels, and may intersect one another. The total length of the tunnels in a naked mole rat colony may be 2.5 miles (4 kilometers). The tunnels connect different kinds of "rooms"—storage rooms, nesting rooms, and even toilet areas.

In some ways, a naked mole rat colony is like a bee colony. There is one queen, and she is the only one that gives birth to young. All the other rats are workers. They take care of the young, search for food, and dig more tunnels and rooms.

A naked mole rat may seem ugly to you, but not to another naked mole rat. They can't really see one another, anyway, because they are nearly blind. They don't need good eyesight because they spend their whole lives in the dark.

*A hyena's teeth
are good for
slashing its prey.*

Chapter Four

Chew on This

Mammals have the most highly developed teeth in the animal world. Each kind of mammal has teeth that are suited to its food supply. In fact, scientists can figure out a lot about a mammal's diet by studying its teeth. Rodents, for instance, have sharp, constantly growing incisors that help them nip off stems. Horses and cows have large flat molars that help them grind up tough grasses. Wolves have long, sharp canine teeth that enable them to slash and hold their **prey**.

Their well-developed teeth are one reason that mammals are so successful. They're equipped to eat all kinds of hard-to-eat foods, ranging from dry grass to hard bones. Yet not all mammals have teeth. You have already learned about some mammals that don't have teeth, including the platypuses, the echidnas, and the pangolins. There are a few others that are also toothless, or nearly so.

A Look at Anteaters

Although an anteater doesn't have a single tooth in its long, tapered snout, and can barely see, it gets along quite nicely. Its long, sticky tongue and excellent sense of smell help it find and eat all the ants it wants.

The giant anteater of South America is the biggest anteater in the world. It can grow up to 7 feet (2.1 m) long from the tip of its snout to the end of its shaggy tail. It spends its waking hours sniffing for ant and termite nests as it shuffles along, with its long fur nearly brushing the ground. Ant and termite nests are almost as hard as rock, but the anteater can easily rip them apart with the powerful claws on its front feet. Once an anteater breaks through the nest walls, it uses its long sticky tongue to reach inside and pick up ants, eggs, and **larvae**.

An anteater's tongue can reach deep into the nest—as far as 24 inches (61 cm). Because it has no teeth, the anteater swallows its food whole. Its tough stomach and strong digestive juices crush and digest its prey. A giant anteater can slurp up as many as 30,000 ants in 1 day.

An anteater looks awkward as it walks along. It curls its long claws under its feet and walks on its wrists. If danger

Such a Tiny Mouth

An anteater's mouth is a small hole no bigger around than a pencil.

A giant anteater has no teeth in its long snout.

The Silky Anteaters

The squirrel-sized silky anteater has soft, golden hair. It hunts for insects in treetops in the tropical forests of South America.

threatens, however, an anteater can run away quickly. If it's cornered, the animal will turn and strike out with its powerful claws. An anteater may look helpless, but it can defend itself from most enemies—even a mountain lion!

In the spring, a female anteater gives birth to a single baby. She carries it around on her back as she hunts for ants. The stripes on the baby's body match the stripes on its mother's back. With that camouflage, most enemies don't even know the baby is there.

All About Aardvarks

An aardvark has just a few teeth in the back of its mouth. It doesn't have very much hair, either. This ant-eating mammal doesn't need a lot of teeth or hair, though. It grinds up its prey in its thick-walled stomach, and its tough skin protects it and helps keep it warm.

The word "aardvark" means "earth pig" in Afrikaans, the language spoken by some people in southern Africa, where aardvarks live. Aardvarks have a piglike snout, and they are excellent diggers. They dig large burrows to rest in during the day. If an enemy attacks while they are hunting at night, they can dig a hiding place in no time. An aardvark can dig a den faster than several people using shovels.

An aardvark can defend itself, too, even though it has so few teeth. If it's cornered, it can sit up on its rump and slash at its attacker with its big front claws. It may also lie on its back and lash out with all four feet.

Aardvarks have excellent senses of hearing and smell. At night, they shuffle along in a zigzag pattern, sniffing and listening for the smells and sounds of termites and ants. Their long, rabbit-like ears turn this way and that, picking up the smallest sounds. They can even hear a column of ants marching along!

*An aardvark
watches for danger
from its burrow.*

The Vanishing Aardvark

Aardvarks were once common in Australia, but now are becoming rare, and human beings are their worst enemies. Many people still hunt aardvarks for their meat, hides, and claws. Farmers kill aardvarks, too, because they think they are pests. The farmers don't realize that aardvarks help them control the termites that destroy crops and grasslands. Some aardvarks are now protected in preserves, but others are still being hunted or driven out of their habitat.

When an aardvark finds a termite mound, it tears into it with its powerful claws. Then it sticks in its long, sticky tongue and quickly laps up every termite it can reach.

Stinging ants don't bother an aardvark. It can close up its ears and nostrils to keep ants out of its snout and ears. Its tough skin protects it from bites and stings. An aardvark may even make a burrow in an ant nest it has just dug up.

A zebra runs across a plain in Tanzania.

Chapter Five

Flying Mammals

Where would you expect to find mammals? You might picture zebras running across the plains of Africa or panthers lurking in the undergrowth. Maybe you think of badgers hiding in their burrows or squirrels leaping about in the trees. Or you may imagine beavers swimming in a pond or whales plowing through the oceans. Most likely, though, you wouldn't think about mammals flying through the air.

If you did, though, you might imagine bats flittering through the night sky as they hunt for insects. Bats are the only mammals that have true wings and fly, but some other mammals can soar through the air. You may have heard of flying squirrels. In Australia, sugar gliders and feathertail gliders glide from branch to branch.

The Bulldog Bat

Most bats hunt insects, and some bats eat fruit. A very few bats suck animal blood. The greater bulldog bat fishes for its dinner!

Like insect-eating bats, a bulldog bat uses **echolocation** to find its prey. This bat gives off high-pitched beeps that bounce back when they hit a ripple in the water. When a fish breaks

This bulldog bat is about to catch a fish.

The Blossom Bat

The blossom bat of New Zealand sips nectar from flowers. It uses its excellent sense of smell to find flowers, then sticks its long snout and even longer tongue inside to lap up nectar. As it flies from flower to flower, it carries pollen on its body. Like bees, blossom bats **pollinate** flowers, helping plants to reproduce.

the surface of the water, the bulldog bat can tell just where it is. It swoops down and grabs the fish with its long curved claws. Then the bat stuffs the fish into its cheek pouches, carries the prey to its roost, and eats it.

People can't hear a bat's beeps with their ears. The sounds that bats make are too fast and high-pitched for us to hear. Scientists need to use special equipment to "hear" the sounds a bat makes. They have learned that in the half second it takes for a bulldog bat to hear and catch its prey, the bat sends out fourteen beeps!

Bulldog bats look a lot like small, flying bulldogs. They live in the steamy rain forests of South America, Mexico, and some islands in the Caribbean. They fish all night, but when day breaks, they fly back to their cave to roost. They live in large groups called colonies. There may be several hundred bats all roosting together in a single cave!

The Sugar Glider

Sugar gliders are well named—they are terrific gliders, and they love sweet things. At first, you might mistake a sugar glider for a flying squirrel. It is about the same size as a flying squirrel, and it glides like one. However, a sugar glider is really a kind of possum, a type of marsupial. Sugar gliders live only in New Guinea, Australia, and nearby islands.

Flaps of thin skin on the sides of the sugar glider's body stretch from its forefeet to its ankles. As it leaps from one branch to another, it spreads its legs wide. The flaps of skin make this animal into a kind of furry hang glider. It steers with its bushy tail. This small creature can glide up to 150 feet (46 m) from one tree to another. That's half the length of a football field!

Sugar gliders love sweets, especially the sweet sap that flows from eucalyptus trees. They also dine on fruit, nectar, and flowers. In the spring and summer, they need extra protein, so they eat insects—mostly beetles and moths.

These small mammals also love each other's company! They nest together in groups of up to seven adults and their

Don't Leave Me Alone!

Sugar gliders need other sugar gliders so much that if one of these small creatures is left alone, it will die of loneliness.

Did You Know?

People who keep sugar gliders as pets say that sugar gliders are very affectionate.

young. The males mark their territory with saliva and with a scent from glands on their body. They also rub their foreheads and chests on other members of the group to mark them with their special scent. All the members of a group have the same scent. That's how they recognize one another.

Most of the time sugar gliders live peacefully together, but there can be problems when outsiders try to enter the group. Sugar gliders don't like outsiders at all! If a stranger comes, the group members know that it smells wrong. They will attack the stranger and chase it away.

Sugar gliders are very vocal. Sometimes they make a "crabbing" noise that sounds like a pencil sharpener. Other times they bark like a puppy to find out where other sugar gliders are. When they're irritated, they make a chattering noise with lots of "s" sounds in it. They sound as if they're swearing at one another!

They're noisy eaters too. They chirp, grunt, and gurgle as they gobble down their food or hunt in tree branches. Sugar gliders have few enemies, so they don't need to be silent to be safe.

Sugar gliders nest together in a bed of leaves.

Feathertail Gliders

If you take a close look at a feathertail glider, you will soon see where it got its name. Its tail looks like a feather, and it is very good at gliding. Its tail hairs grow in an overlapping V-pattern. When a feathertail launches itself from a tree, it spreads out the flaps of skin stretching from its wrists to its knees. Its wonderful feather-like tail helps it steer, so it can change direction easily. A feathertail almost always lands right on the spot it was aiming at.

A feathertail glider glides to a new tree.

Feathertails are talented acrobats too. In fact, their scientific name, *Acrobates pygmaeus*, means "tiny acrobat." They are also excellent climbers. Their first toe is opposable, like a human thumb, which helps them get a good grip on a branch. Their other toes have long, strong claws, which help them hang on.

A feathertail looks a lot like a sugar glider, and it eats the same kinds of food. It especially likes nectar and pollen. The tip of its tongue is like a tiny brush that helps it sip nectar from flowers. It eats a few insects too.

Like sugar gliders, feathertails are social animals. They nest together in groups of up to twenty-five members. Unlike sugar gliders, they don't mark their territories. Feathertails from other places are always welcome to join the group!

Feathertails are the smallest gliding possums. There are several others in the same family, including the largest, the greater glider. It grows up to 32 inches (81 cm) long, and can glide up to 300 feet (91 m). That's twice as far as a sugar glider can go.

Where in the World Are Feathertails?

Feathertails live mostly in the wet, tall forests of eastern Australia. A few live in dry forests.

A baby anteater
clings to its
mother's back.

Chapter Six

Wild Wrap-up

Did you know that there were so many strange mammals in the world? So many of them seem to break the "rules" that you begin to wonder where those rules came from in the first place. Now that you have learned something about some of these strange mammals, you may have different ideas about what a mammal is.

The truth is that there are only a few things that *all* mammals have in common. All mammals are warm-blooded. All have a backbone. Most importantly, all mammals feed their young with mother's milk. So, the next time someone asks you, "What is a mammal?" you might come up with some different answers. You might say, "*Most* mammals give birth to live young," and "*Most* mammals are covered with fur." You might add that "*Most* mammals have well-developed teeth." Then you might go on to describe some of the weird mammals that break all the rules.

Mammal Misfits Around the World

Common name	Scientific name	Where found
Bumblebee bat or Kitti's hog-nosed bat	*Craseonycteris thonglongyai*	Western Thailand
Blue whale	*Balaenoptera musculus*	All oceans
Duck-billed platypus	*Ornithorhynchus anatinus*	Tasmania, southern and eastern Australia
Numbat	*Myrmaecobius fasciatus*	Southwestern Australia
Short-beaked echidna	*Tachyglossus aculeatus*	Australia, Tasmania and New Guinea
Pink fairy armadillo	*Chlamyphorus truncatus*	Sandy plains of Argentina
Three-banded armadillo	*Tolypeutes matacus*	South America
Nine-banded armadillo	*Dasypus novemcinctus*	South and Central America, the south-central and south-eastern United States
Giant pangolin	*Manis gigantea*	Africa, along the equator from West Africa to Uganda
Naked mole rat	*Heterocephalus glaber*	Kenya, Ethiopia and Somalia

Giant anteater	*Myrmecophaga tridactyla*	Southern Belize to northern Argentina
Silky or pygmy anteater	*Cyclopes didactylus*	Forests from Southern Mexico to Bolivia, Brazil
Aardvark	*Orycteropus afer*	Much of sub-Saharan Africa
Mexican bulldog bat or fish-eating bat	*Noctilio leporinus*	Southern Mexico, Argentina, Peru, Brazil, Bahamas, Trinidad, the Antilles
Blossom bat	*Mystacina tuberculata*	New Zealand and nearby islands
Sugar glider	*Petaurus breviceps*	New Guinea and nearby islands, Australia, Tasmania
Feathertail or pygmy glider	*Acrobates pygmaeus*	Eastern Australia

Glossary

camouflage—blending into the surroundings to hide. Some animals have developed special coloring or body shapes to help camouflage themselves.

canine teeth—sharp teeth on the sides of meat-eating animals' jaws that they use to slash and hold prey

carapace—a bony shell on the back of some animals

carnassial teeth—the teeth behind a meat eater's canine teeth. They are used to cut and chew prey.

class—a group of animals that share certain characteristics. The mammals are one class of animals.

colony—a group of animals living together

echolocation—bouncing sounds off objects to find prey or navigate

embryo—an unborn or unhatched animal in an early stage of development

incisors—teeth in the front of an animal's jaws used for nipping or gnawing

incubation period—the time it takes for a newly laid egg to hatch

kingdom—the top-level category for classifying living things. The five kingdoms are plants, animals, protosts, fungi, and bacteria.

larvae—an immature stage of an animal life cycle

mammary gland—one of the glands on the underside of a female mammal that produce milk

marsupials—a group of animals including kangaroos and opossums. Female marsupials carry their young in pouches on their bodies.

monotreme—an egg-laying mammal, such as a platypus or an echidna

nocturnal—active at night

order—a group of animals within a class that share certain characteristics

placenta—a structure filled with blood vessels that nourishes an embryo while it is still in its mother's uterus

pollinate—to fertilize a plant for reproduction

pore—a small hole in the skin

predator—an animal that hunts another animal

prey—an animal hunted by another animal for food

taxonomy—the science of organizing living things into categories

uterus—an organ inside a female mammal where embryos develop

venom—a poisonous liquid produced by an animal

vertebrate—an animal that has a backbone

warm-blooded—an animal that can regulate its own internal body temperature

To Find Out More

Books

Burnie, David. *Eyewitness Explorers: Mammals*. New York: DK
   Publishing, 1998.

Elliott, Leslie. *Mind-Blowing Mammals*. New York: Sterling
   Publications, 1994.

Lovett, Sarah. *Extremely Weird Mammals*. Santa Fe, NM: John
   Muir Publications, 1996.

Moser, Madeline. *Ever Heard of an Aardwolf?: A Miscellany of
   Uncommon Animals*. San Diego: Harcourt Brace, 1996.

Ricciuti, Edward R. *What on Earth Is a Pangolin?* Woodbridge,
   CT: Blackbirch Press, 1994.

Short, Joan. *Platypus*. Greenvale, NY: Mondo Publishing, 1997.

Tesar, Jenny E. *Echidna*. Woodbridge, CT: Blackbirch Press, 1995.

Organizations and Online Sites

Animals—Australia
http://www.ozramp.net.au/~senani/animaust.htm
This site is devoted to Australian animals, including platypuses and echidnas.

The Animal Diversity Web
http://www.oit.itd.umich.edu/bio/
This site contains information about individual species in several different classes of animals, including mammals.

Animal Info: Rare, Threatened and Endangered Mammals
http://www.animalinfo.org
This site provides detailed information about threatened and endangered mammals, including a list of the world's rarest mammals.

Bat Conservation International
http://www.batcon.org
This group provides factual information about the often misunderstood bats of the world.

A Note on Sources

The first thing I did when I began work on this book was to dig into my memory. Over the years, I have taken numerous courses in natural history and visited dozens of zoos and nature preserves around the world. Thinking about those experiences gave me more ideas for strange mammals to include.

My next step was to browse through my personal nature library. The National Geographic Society's *Book of Mammals* is a very helpful source. It comes in two volumes and has excellent descriptions of mammals all around the world. A textbook from a graduate school mammalogy course, *Mammalogy* (Terry A. Vaughan), was invaluable in helping me check specific facts, including dentition and other details. I supplemented my own books with others from the local libraries.

Finally, once I decided which species I wanted to include, I went to the Internet. By plugging in the genus and species, I was often able to find useful information, particularly in sites posted by universities and zoos. My favorite site for mammals is *The Animal Diversity Web* from the biology department at the University of Michigan. Their information is both accurate and up-to-date, and they're worth checking out, no matter what mammal you're interested in.

The help of expert consultant Kathy Carlstead, Ph.D., of the Honolulu Zoo in Honolulu, Hawaii, was invaluable in creating this book.

—*Sara Swan Miller*

Index

Numbers in *italics* indicate illustrations.

About the Author

Sara Swan Miller has enjoyed working with children all her life, first as a Montessori nursery-school teacher and later as an outdoor environmental educator at the Mohonk Preserve in New Paltz, New York. As director of the school program, she has taught hundreds of children on the importance of appreciating the natural world.

She has written more than 30 books, including *Three Stories You Can Read to Your Dog*; *Three Stories You Can Read to Your Cat*; *Three* More *Stories You Can Read to Your Dog*; and *What's in the Woods? An Outdoor Activity Book*; as well as four other books on strange animals for the Watts Library. She has also written several True Books on farm animals for Children's Press, and more than a dozen books for Franklin Watts' Animals in Order series.